IF FO

👤 _____

✉ _____

📱 _____

Greater Than a Tourist Book Series Reviews from Readers

I think the series is wonderful and beneficial for tourists to get information before visiting the city.

-Seckin Zumbul, Izmir Turkey

I am a world traveler who has read many trip guides but this one really made a difference for me. I would call it a heartfelt creation of a local guide expert instead of just a guide.

-Susy, Isla Holbox, Mexico

New to the area like me, this is a must have!

-Joe, Bloomington, USA

This is a good series that gets down to it when looking for things to do at your destination without having to read a novel for just a few ideas.

-Rachel, Monterey, USA

Good information to have to plan my trip to this destination.

-Pennie Farrell, Mexico

Great ideas for a port day.

-Mary Martin USA

Aptly titled, you won't just be a tourist after reading this book. You'll be greater than a tourist!

-Alan Warner, Grand Rapids, USA

Even though I only have three days to spend in San Miguel in an upcoming visit, I will use the author's suggestions to guide some of my time there. An easy read - with chapters named to guide me in directions I want to go.

 -Robert Catapano, USA

Great insights from a local perspective! Useful information and a very good value!

 -Sarah, USA

This series provides an in-depth experience through the eyes of a local. Reading these series will help you to travel the city in with confidence and it'll make your journey a unique one.

-Andrew Teoh, Ipoh, Malaysia

>TOURIST

GREATER THAN A TOURIST- SCOTTSDALE ARIZONA USA

50 Travel Tips from a Local

Julia McDonnell

Greater Than a Tourist- Scottsdale Arizona USA Copyright © 2018 by CZYK Publishing LLC. All Rights Reserved.

All rights reserved. No part of this book may be reproduced in any form or by any electronic or mechanical means including information storage and retrieval systems, without permission in writing from the author. The only exception is by a reviewer, who may quote short excerpts in a review.

The statements in this book are of the authors and may not be the views of CZYK Publishing or Greater Than a Tourist.

Cover designed by: Ivana Stamenkovic
Cover Image: https://pixabay.com/en/arizona-pinnacle-peak-hiking-2449840/

CZYK Publishing Since 2011.

Greater Than a Tourist
Visit our website at www.GreaterThanaTourist.com

Lock Haven, PA
All rights reserved.
ISBN: 9781791536718

>TOURIST
50 TRAVEL TIPS FROM A LOCAL

BOOK DESCRIPTION

Are you excited about planning your next trip?

Do you want to try something new?

Would you like some guidance from a local?

If you answered yes to any of these questions, then this Greater Than a Tourist book is for you.

Greater Than a Tourist – Scottsdale Arizona USA by Julia McDonnell offers the inside scoop on Scottsdale. Most travel books tell you how to travel like a tourist. Although there is nothing wrong with that, as part of the Greater Than a Tourist series, this book will give you travel tips from someone who has lived at your next travel destination.

In these pages, you will discover advice that will help you throughout your stay. This book will not tell you exact addresses or store hours but instead will give you excitement and knowledge from a local that you may not find in other smaller print travel books.

Travel like a local. Slow down, stay in one place, and get to know the people and the culture. By the time you finish this book, you will be eager and prepared to travel to your next destination.

TABLE OF CONTENTS

BOOK DESCRIPTION
TABLE OF CONTENTS
DEDICATION
ABOUT THE AUTHOR
HOW TO USE THIS BOOK
FROM THE PUBLISHER
OUR STORY
WELCOME TO
> TOURIST
INTRODUCTION
1. Before You Arrive
2. Pet-Friendly
3. Getting Here
4. Getting Around
5. Free Rides
6. The Lay of the Town
7. Weather
8. Water And Sunscreen
9. Old Town Scottsdale
10. Cartel Coffee Lab
11. Origianl ChopShop
12. Oregano's Pizza Bistro
13. Citizen Public House
14. The Poisoned Pen

15. ArtWak
16. Scottsdale Historical Museum
17. Surprising Contemporary Discovery
18. Knights Rise At SMoCA
19. Eat, Drink, And Be Merry
20. Merci French Cafe & Patisserie - If You Please!
21. Underground Seafood?
22. Wildflower (Bread Company)
23. Taliesin West - Frank Lloyd Wright
24. Frank Lloyd Wright Spire
25. Cosanti - Paolo Soleri
26. Arcosanit
27. Ride The Rails
28. Car Crazy
29. Cars And Coffee
30. Penske Race Museum
31. More Cars At The Pavilions
32. Horsepower Of The Four-Legged Kind
33. MacDonald's Ranch
34. Fresh Air And Sunshine
35. Papago Park
36. Desert Botanical Gardens
37. Gertrude's At The Gardens
38. Indian Bend Wash
39. Singh Meadows
40. Hiking, Biking, And Horseback Riding

>TOURIST

41. Scottsdale Waterfront
42. Scottsdale Public Art Walk
43. Soleri Bridge And Copper Falls
44. Fun Festivals
45. Canal Convergence
46. Fun And Games
47. Phoenix Open In Scottsdale
48. Baseball Buzz
49. SkySong
50. Hot Times Cool Fun

TOP REASONS TO BOOK THIS TRIP

50 THINGS TO KNOW ABOUT PACKING LIGHT FOR TRAVEL

Packing and Planning Tips

Travel Questions

Travel Bucket List

NOTES

DEDICATION

This book is dedicated to my family for all their love and support.

ABOUT THE AUTHOR

Julia McDonnell has lived most of her life in the American Southwest while traveling extensively througout the country, across the borders into Canada and Mexico, and throughout Europe. Her wanderlust is fueled by her passion for exploring, discovering and experiencing fun places, great food and new adventures. She and her husband Tommy are longtime residents of Arizona, currently living in Tempe.

HOW TO USE THIS BOOK

The Greater Than a Tourist book series was written by someone who has lived in an area for over three months. The goal of this book is to help travelers either dream or experience different locations by providing opinions from a local. The author has made suggestions based on their own experiences. Please do your own research before traveling to the area in case the suggested places are unavailable.

Travel Advisories: As a first step in planning any trip abroad, check the Travel Advisories for your intended destination.
https://travel.state.gov/content/travel/en/traveladvisories/traveladvisories.html

FROM THE PUBLISHER

Traveling can be one of the most important parts of a person's life. The anticipation and memories that you have are some of the best. As a publisher of the Greater Than a Tourist book series, as well as the popular 50 Things to Know book series, we strive to help you learn about new places, spark your imagination, and inspire you. Wherever you are and whatever you do I wish you safe, fun, and inspiring travel.

Lisa Rusczyk Ed. D.
CZYK Publishing

OUR STORY

Traveling is a passion of the "Greater than a Tourist" series creator. Lisa studied abroad in college, and for their honeymoon Lisa and her husband toured Europe. During her travels to Malta, an older man tried to give her some advice based on his own experience living on the island since he was a young boy. She was not sure if she should talk to the stranger but was interested in his advice. When traveling to some places she was wary to talk to locals because she was afraid that they weren't being genuine. Through her travels, Lisa learned how much locals had to share with tourists. Lisa created the "Greater Than a Tourist" book series to help connect people with locals. A topic that locals are very passionate about sharing.

>TOURIST

WELCOME TO
> TOURIST

INTRODUCTION

"Travel. As much as you can. As far as you can. As long as you can. Life's not meant to be lived in one place."

— Unknown

DESTINATION: SCOTTSDALE, ARIZONA!

Visiting Scottsdale any time of the year is an opportunity for fun-filled activities and adventures. This jewel of a city in the Sonoran Desert is a year-round destination for sun seekers, fun seekers and all around pleasure seekers. Whether it is recreation, relaxation, or respite from the winter cold you are seeking, Scottsdale offers more than enough entertainment to satisfy all ages any time of the year.

Hosting several annual events, Scottsdale is a hotbed of activity, drawing huge crowds of visitors during the winter months. It is also a popular destination for conventions and conferences as well as vacations and outdoor recreation becoming a year-round destination.

Located in the northeastern section of the Greater Phoenix Area (the Valley), and bordering the McDowell Mountain Range and Tonto National Forest, Scottsdale is abundant with activities, adventure, arts and culture, entertainment, fine dining, personal pampering and plenty of sunshine!

You name it; there is something for everyone making Scottsdale, Arizona a top-of-the-list stay and play destination.

1. BEFORE YOU ARRIVE

Plan as far ahead as possible, especially if you want to visit during peak season.

Annual events draw huge crowds. Accommodations fill up quickly, so make reservations as early as possible. Think ahead about other activities as well, especially dining, if you have your heart set on a specific restaurant. Make reservations as soon as the establishment will accept them.

Rates are higher during the winter months when visitors are flocking in to enjoy the mild weather and attend special events. Consider a summer visit. Summertime heat helps bring rates down and availability goes up.

If you plan to travel with your pet, consider your activities and entertainment options before arriving. Some hiking and biking trails and events restrict animals. Leaving a pet in a hotel room is not always an option and finding a kennel or sitter might be challenging and require reservations. However, some resorts offer accomodations or at least suggestions for pet care - check in advance..

2. PET-FRIENDLY

Scottsdale is a generally a pet-friendly city and pets are welcome almost everywhere. Many restaurants and bars have pet-friendly patios and offer water bowls and sometimes even treats for your furry friends.

Pets are welcome to join you on most trails and pathways as well as long your pets are leashed and you clean up after them.

Some locations and activities have special dog-days (or nights) such as Desert Botanic Gardens and Chase Field (baseball park in downtown Phoenix and home of the Arizona Diamondbacks) allowing you to share the activity with your pet at your side. There are also numerous dog parks where your furry friend can run free.

The desert, however, can be less than friendly, especially as the temperatures rise. Pets are as susceptible to the heat as people are and need to be given particular attention. Always have extra water for pets and be very watchful of how hot the pavement is. If you can't walk barefoot, neither should your pet. Never leave an animal in a vehicle - ever! Even in the winter. There are laws prohibiting

>TOURIST

animals being left in vehicles at any time for any amount of time.

Always check ahead to make sure dogs are welcome and make your plans accordingly.

3. GETTING HERE

Scottsdale has an airport if you have access to a private plane. Located about 9 miles north of downtown Scottsdale, this small one-runway airport is busy with private aviation. As yet, there are no commercial flights. You might find a charter.

Phoenix International airport (Sky Harbor) serves the greater Phoenix area and is conveniently located just minutes away, about 10 miles, from downtown Scottsdale and is easily accessed with a rental car or hired driver.

If you are driving to Scottsdale, it is easy to arrive via major highways. Interstates 10 and 17 connect with Arizona State Route 101 (or Loop 101) which will take you around the north and east of Scottsdale. State Route 202 (Loop 202) a partial beltway south of Scottsdale. connects with Loop 101.

4. GETTING AROUND

So! You are in Scottsdale.

Once you have arrived in Scottsdale, you can stay and play quite easily with little need of a vehicle for transportation.

If you are staying close to downtown, many of the activities, entertainment and eateries are easily accessible and in walking or biking distance. There are also Pedi-cabs and even horse-drawn carriages in the cooler temperatures in Old Town.

Most of the annual events that take place further out from downtown have plenty of parking and provide shuttles to help minimize traffic and parking congestion as well as ease of getting to the entrances.

5. FREE RIDES

Hop on and off the Scottsdale Trolly for FREE rides around the downtown area. These colorful trolleys, reminiscent of old Cable and Trolley Cars, serve an expanded area with four free routes around Old Town and into nearby neighborhoods. Routes connect with valley-wide city transit buses using

>TOURIST

some of the same stops. Schedules vary by the route and day. Service is daily except for major holidays.

Many of the 'trolleys' are now decorated city transit-sized buses with air-conditioning. They are wheelchair-accessible and will take your bicycle, too. Dogs are not allowed.

6. THE LAY OF THE TOWN

Streets, Avenues, Boulevards, Roads, names, numbers — a bit of confusion

Even with a GPS, I like to be familiar with the lay of a town. Ok, I admit it, I am a map-reader, and I want to see how the streets layout. I am also cautious as I've experienced some misguidance when the GPS is a bit off at times, so I like to have an idea of where I am going and where the GPS is supposed to be taking me.

Downtown and Old Town are one and the same. This area is where the city has its origins. Main Street separates the streets (south) and the avenues (north). North Scottsdale Rd (there is no South Scottsdale Rd) is the major thoroughfare all the way through Scottsdale with North Hayden Rd to the east.

Goldwater Blvd to the west and Drinkwater Blvd to the east are convenient routes to by-pass the busy Old Town area.

All other north-south streets are numbered from west to east, and all east-west roads have names (Thomas, Osborn, Indian School, Camelback, etc.)

7. WEATHER

Folks like U.S. Army Chaplain Winfield Scott and his brother George have been flocking to Scottsdale since the mid 1800s, attracted by the climate and the opportunities it provids.

Winters are mild to warm, although a bit of frost - even a dusting of snow - once in a while reminds us why we live here and can appreciate the summer heat.

Summers are hot. Well, ok - HOT! How hot is hot? Some say extremely hot while others say scorching! It all depends on your tolerance.

During summer visits, enjoy water play or sitting poolside with a refreshing cold drink in hand during the heat of the day and keep your outdoor activities to early mornings and late evenings. Mid-day is a good time for air-conditioned indoor entertainment —

museums, shopping, movies. It is an excellent time to visit OdySea Aquarium and the Butterfly Pavillion.

With summer comes the desert 'monsoon' season when the humidity rises along with the heat, but few rain showers develop. Occasionally there will be a true 'gully washer' so be cautious of flash floods anywhere but especially if you are out in the desert.

8. WATER AND SUNSCREEN

Always have water with you, and drink extra! Your body will need more water than you might think - even in the winter. Take adequate water with you for outdoor recreation especially the more strenuous activities like jogging, biking, and hiking. Adequate means more than you think you'll drink. You also want extra water when playing golf or just walking around town. Enjoy your beer, wine, and other libations, even coffee and tea, but quench your thirst and refresh yourself with water!

Slather on the sunscreen! The sun is the sun, any time of the year. During the winter as you enjoy the warmth, you should still wear sunscreen and possibly have a hat with you, especially for those outdoor activities and recreation, including that innocent walk around town.

9. OLD TOWN SCOTTSDALE

Downtown and Old Town Scottsdale are the same. The original location of the town of Scottsdale, it continues to be the heart of the city. It's where the action - is with an exciting and entertaining mix of art galleries, boutiques, gift shops, and museums. There are more than enough food and drink establishments to satisfy your hunger and satiate your thirst.

The boardwalk in Old Town gives a real western feel to the downtown area and underscores the city's slogan, "The West's Most Western Town."

Many shops are western-themed with buckles and belts, boots and bolo ties, and blankets. You will find handmade turquoise and silver jewelry, pottery, and Indian artifacts. Beautiful galleries and boutiques offer western artwork and collectibles alongside traditional and contemporary pieces of art.

Some of the shops are family owned and have historical connections with Scottsdale. Saba Western Wear and Gilbert Ortega Native American Galleries have been passed down through several generations.

>TOURIST

Old Town Scottsdale offers hours, even days, of entertainment any time of the day or night and any time of the year --enough to make you want to stay and play just in Old Town - even during the heat of summer.

Be aware that once the weather starts cooling off, the crowds start increasing all over Scottsdale, especially in Old Town. I think it's exciting - the more, the merrier!

Eat and Drink and Shop to your heart's content in Old Town.

10. CARTEL COFFEE LAB

After wandering along the boardwalk and browsing the galleries and shops, the irresistible and intoxicating aroma of freshly roasted coffee beans draws me into Cartel Coffee Lab on 5th Ave, west of Scottsdale Rd, for my favorite Cappuccino with its artistic design in the foam.

Cartel is a locally owned coffee house serving coffee made from fair trade-sourced coffee beans, freshly roasted in-house at the original Tempe location. Cartel coffee is rich in flavor and aroma and perfect for lingering over while people-watching on the boardwalk

11. ORIGIANL CHOPSHOP

Of the myriad choices of eateries in Old Town, my go-to, for flavorful, healthy, and always satisfying 'Feel Good Food' (their motto) is the Original Chop Shop at the corner of 5th Ave and N Scottsdale Rd, just east of Cartel Coffee.

An Arizona based restaurant, the Original Chop Shop offers a selection of delicious foods crafted with wholesome ingredients. Some of my menu favs are the Danish Salad, Terriaki Chicken, Jacked Up PB&J Protein Shake and the Acai Bowl (my first ever and still top of the list after tasting others). Of course, menus can change, but so far, everything I've had on this menu is worth a repeat visit!

12. OREGANO'S PIZZA BISTRO

Besides fresh roasting coffee beans and fresh buttery popcorn, what perks up your senses and stimulates your appetite more than anything else? Garlic butter, herbs, and tomatoes! Try walking past

>TOURIST

Oregano's and ignoring their tantalizing aroma of garlic butter and pizza sauce.

There are plenty of great pizzas in town, but I think Oregano's is extra special. Thin crust, deep-dish, (Pan) or double crust (Stuffed Pizza) - take your pick. I go for their Chicago Style Pan Pizza (deep-dish) filled with gooey stringy (real) cheese, savory, garlicky tomato sauce, and any other favorite 'toppings' (or fillings) of your choice. It takes a bit longer to cook, but is worth the wait.

While waiting, enjoy a cold beer or one of their specialty drinks (non-alcoholic included) with some Kick Butt Garlic Bread or Boom Dip.

Once inside and perusing the menu, you may be tempted by something other than pizza - that's ok - it's ALL delicious!

Oregano's is another locally owned 'chain' restaurant with several locations in the valley. Most have outside seating. I am partial to the patio at the Scottsdale store, located south of Old Town on Scottsdale Rd at Earl, between Thomas and the Drinkwater bypass.

13. CITIZEN PUBLIC HOUSE

Is it possible to be elegant and casual at the same time?

I think of this as a fancy pub experience in Old Town. Citizen Public House on 5th Avenue is unique. It is a little more upscale, white tablecloths and such (and prices reflect that) while being a relaxed and casual atmosphere.

The menu is considered 'new American' which is basically well-crafted versions of standard fare. I can only speak about The Original Chopped Salad.

Everyone seems to love the chopped salad. In fact, it is so popular it even has it's own Facebook Page!

What makes it so good is difficult to determine. The ingredients seem innocent enough: Smoked salmon, Israeli couscous, arugula, pepitas, Asiago cheese, black currants, dried sweet corn, marinated tomatoes with a buttermilk-herb dressing. Apparently, it is the right combination that comes together for an incredible culinary experience! (unless they use a super secret ingredient). The salad is mixed tableside so that secret ingredient must be hidden in the dressing or tomato marinade. Perhaps it is a sleight of hand?

Choose an Arizona Brewery draft beer (it is a pub after all) or one of the unique house cocktails (barrel-aged) and enjoy your evening.

Open 4 p.m. - 11 p.m. (midnight Fri & Sat) with a social hour 4 pm. - 6 p.m. seven days a week. Located at 7111 E 5th Ave

14. THE POISONED PEN

For bookworms like me, The Poisoned Pen is a favorite place. I love books and, and this quaint little shop in Old Town is delightful. I easily 'get lost' while perusing the mysteries, adventures, and stories of intrigue.

This small bookstore is home to two of my favorite authors, Clive Cussler (Dirk Pit series) and Diana Gabaldon (Outlander series), both Scottsdale residents, who frequent the shop and offer book signings.

There is always something happening at this charming little bookstore. Check their extensive calendar of events online to learn who and what might be scheduled while you are visiting Scottsdale. Perhaps your favorite author will be there, or you might discover a new 'favorite' at the Poisoned Pen.

Visit this beautiful bookshop any time for a unique bookstore experience!

15. ARTWAK

Some events in Scottsdale are monthly; others are twice a year, some are annually. ArtWalk in Old Town Scottsdale is WEEKLY.

Held every Thursday evening - year round except Thanksgiving - from 7-9 p.m. This FREE event is hosted by the Scottsdale Gallery Association (a non-profit) and takes place in Old Town.

Stroll along the sidewalks, wander in and out of galleries, have a bite to eat and perhaps a glass of wine. Shops are open late, and some galleries offer complimentary refreshments.

I especially enjoy this excuse to be out in the evening air, casually passing the time, viewing the art galleries and people watching. Find a bench or sit outside on a patio and enjoy the evening. Stroll over to SCoMA for a view of the night sky from Knights Rise. Any time of the year, ArtWalk is a wonderful opportunity to enjoy Old Town.

>TOURIST

16. SCOTTSDALE HISTORICAL MUSEUM

The historic Little Red School House was built in 1909 and is now the home of the Scottsdale Historical Museum. Located in the Old Town district, this fun museum exhibits photos, artifacts, and historical records providing a fascinating view of the history and development of Scottsdale and the surrounding area.

This is another FREE activity. It is closed in the summer, June-August.

17. SURPRISING CONTEMPORARY DISCOVERY

Museums are always intriguing to me; however, I often skip the modern and contemporary artworks, going for the more traditional pieces, which is probably why the Scottsdale Museum of Contemporary Art was out of my radar for a long time. I was pleasantly surprised when I finally 'discovered' it on the edge of the arts district in Old Town.

This museum seems to blend quietly into its surroundings. And yet, with the contemporary exterior design, I should have been intrigued a long time ago!

The building is a creative retrofit of an old movie theater, by award-winning local architect, Will Bruder. A unique curved wall of translucent glass panels encloses one side of the building allowing diffused light and images of the exterior landscape into the sculpture garden ad courtyard; creating a sense of privacy from the outside world. A piece of art on its own, this Glass Scrim Wall becomes an extension of the sculpture garden it encloses.

The artisitc and creative designs contintues within courtyard with plants nad natural lighting. I was thrilled to see a 'chandelier' of bronze bells by the late Arizona artist and architect Paolo Soleri.

The courtyard and sculpture garden are a part of and yet separate from the museum with FREE access through the lobby.

The museum itself is small with only a few exhibits at any one time, often featuring local artists and including architectural and design exhibits as well as modern and contemporary displays.

SMoCA, as you will often see this museum referred to, is FREE all day Thursday during the weekly ArtWalk In Old Town. The museum is also FREE 5 p.m. - 9 p.m. every Saturday and Sunday.

18. KNIGHTS RISE AT SMOCA

A visit to Knights Rise at the Scottsdale Museum of Contemporary Art IN Old Town is a must and FREE. This permanent installation is currently one of only 14 of Arizona-based artist James Turrell's 'skyspaces' open to the public in the United States.

Walk through the sculpture garden and atrium around the museum into an intriguing conically shaped room of cement with an opening at the top that draws your attention to a captivating view of the sky. Benches formed around the room provide seating for visitors to sit and gaze at the sky through the opening, pondering different effects from changes in light, clouds, and even a random bird or airplane flying over the skyspace. The perspectives and experiences of Knights Rise skyspace are unique to each day and each viewer.

I find it mesmerizing ….

19. EAT, DRINK, AND BE MERRY

With the multitude of restaurants, bars, and pubs in Scottsdale, you will quickly and easily find any food and drink of your preference. I like to support local businesses. However, national chain restaurants and bars are well represented here. From basic burgers to fancy fish, and from coffee to craft beers, you will find your favorite foods. The challenge will be making a choice.

20. MERCI FRENCH CAFE & PATISSERIE - IF YOU PLEASE!

A truly authentic and quaint little Mom and Pop French café and patisserie, (Mom and Pop are from Paris!) Merci offers an exquisite array of pastries and decadent desserts, traditional Macarons and Madeleines, and delicious French cuisine in a casual and friendly atmosphere. Breakfast and lunch are served daily with limited days and hours for dinner. Take out is available.

Be there early to get one of the authentic Pain Au Chocolate (chocolate croissants) baked fresh daily from dough imported from France. If you miss the

Pain Au Chocolate, you might still have a choice of equally delicious and flaky butter, almond, or raisin croissants.

Often, while relishing a Pain Au Chocolate and a large cup of delicious steaming coffee (their house blend which is so good I buy for brewing at home), I am tempted by the mouthwatering aroma of Quiche, Eggs Benedict, or Croque Madam (with egg) or Monsieur (without egg) and splurge on breakfast or lunch. All of the breakfast menu items are equally delectable. To date, the club sandwich tops my list for lunch. For dinner? Well, the mussels, duck l'orange, and cod are my favorites. However, the chef's special is always worth having. The burgers look amazing, and the classic escargot and frog legs are favorites with many patrons.

Order at the register, help yourself to chilled water, and find a table on the pet-friendly patio or stay inside and enjoy the friendly French ambiance.

Just a short distance from the heart of bustling Old Town, Merci is tucked on one end of a strip-mall (on the corner of E Indian School Rd and N Miller Rd) with a Free Trolley stop right there on Miller.

21. UNDERGROUND SEAFOOD?

Does fresh seafood - in the desert - in a cellar - sound a little 'fishy' ? It might - until you experience the freshest of fresh seafood in this desert - three flights underground Scottsdale at The Salt Cellar Restaurant.

Located on the south end of Hayden Rd just north of McKellips Rd (complete opposite end from Wildflower Bread Company on the north end), this unique dining experience is a must! Known since 1971 for the freshness of their seafood and the refreshingly simple yet delectable preparation of all menu items, the Salt Cellar is a premium culinary adventure /experience!

For fresh seafood in the desert, expect to pay a pretty price. However you can enjoy the experience and not break the bank since all appetizers are available after 4 p.m. at the bar; and discounted cocktails and a special appetizer menu during their 'Twin' Happy Hours from 4 p.m.-7 p.m. and 10 p.m - close.

As in many establishments in Scottsdale, the atmosphere is classy yet casual. Reservations are accepted, not required, but I recommend them - why chance it?

>TOURIST

22. WILDFLOWER (BREAD COMPANY)

Wildflower is my go-to for comfort food. It is consistent, delicious, and always available.

Locally owned, with several locations in the greater Phoenix area, you will find Wildflower in North Scottsdale in the Sonora Village shopping center on North Hayden Rd and Frank Lloyd Wright Blvd west of Highway 101.

Everything I have eaten at Wildflower has been great and making a choice is always difficult. My favorites are the Chopped Salad with salmon (chicken is an option), and the Portabella Picnic sandwich. Salmon Alfredo is my favorite of the pasta dishes with Butternut Squash Ravioli, Pasta Primavera, and Rosemary Chicken close rivals. The menu changes slightly with seasonal favorites like the Turkey Cranberry Walnut Stuffing Sandwich.

I always bring out-of-town visitors here, and they rave about it, requesting a return visit the next time they are in town. Fortunately, I get to return often and have been eating my way through the menu, which is challenging with new and seasonal items distracting me.

It IS a Bread Company, so pick up a baguette or one of their other fresh baked bread items and desserts for your picnic in the park or a day's outing. Their 'Bread of the Month' gives a bit of mix-up to the daily choices; however, my staple is their Rosemary Sea Salt bread for anytime goodness.

Order at the counter, take your drink and order number and find a seat. In short order, your food and flatware are delivered to your table

Wildflower has excellent food, efficient and friendly service, and a comfortable atmosphere. And it is open for breakfast, lunch, and dinner.

23. TALIESIN WEST – FRANK LLOYD WRIGHT

The designs and concepts of world-renowned architect Frank Lloyd Wright have fascinated me since childhood. It was an exciting day for me when I finally had an opportunity to visit Taliesin West, to walk into his buildings, his winter home, and to see his workspace in person.

Wright was one of the first artists and architects to be inspired by the beauty of the desert and one of the first "snowbirds" to make an annual trek away from the cold to the mild weather of Arizona

An Arizona treasure and a National Historic Landmark, Taliesin West was built by Mr. Wright and his apprentices in the 1930s as their winter residence, studio, and educational facility.

Mr. Wright chose to build Taliesin West in the foothills of the McDowell Mountains near Scottsdale, over the hill and out of sight of the city of Phoenix. He used rocks and sand gathered from the area to balance and blend his designs with nature and the environment.

The lights of the city are no longer out of sight, with the encroachment of an expanding Scottsdale. However, Taliesin West retains the unique environmental concepts of Frank Lloyd Wright. It continues to be an active architectural community as the main campus of the School of Architecture at Taliesin and is home to the Frank Lloyd Wright Foundation.

Taliesin West is open to the public with a variety of tours available. Cost varies on the type of tour. Reservations are strongly recommended.

24. FRANK LLOYD WRIGHT SPIRE

Either on the way to Taliesin West or returning from, be sure to at least drive by the FLW Spire the corner of N Scottsdale Rd and Frank Lloyd Wright Blvd.

Better yet, park and visit the plaza where this stunning monument stands surrounded by fountains, other sculptures, and artifacts of Frank Lloyd Wright.

Initially conceived by FLW in the 1950s, the City of Scottsdale finally erected this magnificent spire. Constructed of steel and glass, it reaches 125 feet toward the sky. Colored a bright blue, reminiscent of the turquoise found in Arizona, at night it glows blue from large lights on the inside.

A tall pointed blue spire jutting out of the ground might seem bizarre and out of line with Frank Lloyd Wright's concepts of blending natural colors and surrounding landscape.

Look again. And consider how the spire points up into the sky blending with and disappearing into it.

>TOURIST

25. COSANTI – PAOLO SOLERI

Another Arizona treasure and one of my favorite places to visit is this intriguing artist compound designed and built by Italian-born artist and architect, Paolo Soleri. I go for the bells...and for the brief respite I experience in their tranquil setting. The bells are great for gifts, and I occasionally allow myself to add another one to my own collection. I also like to visit just to hang out, wander around and ring the bells!

Cosanti is located a few miles west of Taliesin West, on Doubletree Ranch Rd west of Scottsdale Rd. This Arizona Historic Site is a collection of unique earth-formed concrete structures. They house a gift shop, galleries, residences, and a working foundry. Natural landscaping creates a peaceful and tranquil space with courtyards, garden paths and galleries filled with ceramic and bronze bells for sale.

When driving to Cosanti, watch carefully for the unassuming entrance - a bit unexpected amidst the upscale neighborhood homes. Turning off a busy street into a shaded gravel parking lot, one immediately feels the tranquility of Cosanti.

After studying with Frank Lloyd Wright in the mid-1940s, Soleri returned to Scottsdale and established Cosanti as his residence, studio, and location for his experimental structures and foundry for ceramic and bronze bells.

Cosanti is open to the public daily except for major holidays. It costs nothing to enter but it usually costs me to leave… bell in hand!

Call ahead for hours and tour times (and cost of tours and demonstrations). Daily guided tours and foundry demonstrations are available weekdays only. Customized guided tours are by reservation.

If your visit is timely, you may get to watch a 'pouring' of bronze bells!

26. ARCOSANIT

For fun extended day's outing away from the city, I like to go to Arcosanti. This fascinating commune is part of Paolo Soleri's futuristic urban design concept for high-density living. For a more in-depth understanding of this fascinating artist, architect, author, lecturer, and philosopher, view exhibits of his concepts and designs. Tour the grounds (donation fee), eat in the cafeteria… and buy more bells!

Travel north of Phoenix on I-17 to Cordes Junction (about 70 miles), exit and follow signs for

Arcosanti—visible after a short distance on a dirt road. Leave pets behind as they are not allowed in the compound and never allowed to be left in vehicles.

27. RIDE THE RAILS

Or just picnic while enjoying the acres of lawn at McCormick-Stillman Railroad Park.

A destination of its own, this railroad-themed park is where young and old get to play, dream, and experience the world of trains and railroads. The vast 40-acre park offers beautiful lawns for picnics and playing.

Ride the miniature train (big enough for adults!) through the park and xeriscape arboretum, across trestles and through tunnels.

Wander the grounds and view the full-sized historic train cars and old depot buildings. Ride the carousel. Visit the museum. Watch the trains traveling through a myriad of tracks and scenery in Model Train Clubs' exhibit in the old McCormick Ranch bunkhouse.

Bring a picnic and your chairs or sit on your blanket on the ground and enjoy the gorgeous weather and FREE concerts-in-the park on Sunday evenings through June

The park and the model train exhibit are FREE. Tickets to ride the train and carousel and visit the museum are a nominal cost.

The park is located at the southeast corner of Scottsdale Road and Indian Bend Road and is open every day of the year except Thanksgiving and Christmas.

28. CAR CRAZY

Scottsdale is a hub of automobile activity. People here are crazy for cars! At one time or another, you will see anything and everything automotive in Scottsdale. From vintage and classic collectibles to exotic, exquisite and extremely expensive vehicles, they are out and about on the streets in Scottsdale.

For an over-dose of car craze and automobilia, join the hundreds of thousands of visitors who descend on Scottsdale each year in mid-January to view hundreds of thousands of dollars worth of vehicles that are up for auction, on display and driving around town.

Choose from the world-famous Barrett-Jackson and Russo-Steele Auctions to several other lesser

>TOURIST

known but equally exciting automobile activity. Gooding & Company, Bonhams, RM Sothebys, Worldwide Auctioneer Scottsdale Auction, and Silver Auctions Arizona all join the fun - or is it a frenzy? and get their piece of the action.

But why choose? Take them all in. If you juggle your timing just right, between the smaller one- and two-day auctions and the longest running, Barrett-Jackson, you might be able to see action at all of them.

This crazy car week might seem a bit daunting, but if you are the least bit interested in vehicles, you will enjoy the excitement and anticipation of this phenomenal experience and should give it a go at least once in your lifetime!

29. CARS AND COFFEE

Still car crazy after all those auctions? Or perhaps you weren't able to attend the annual auto week?

Scottsdale Motorsports Gathering, known as Cars and Coffee is another opportunity to see some beautiful vehicles. Even if you are only slightly passionate about cars or have a mild intrigue, you might want to take in Cars and Coffee.

All cars are welcome; however the focus is on rare high performance and collector cars. This is where you get to see Ferraris, Lamborghinis, and McLarens by the dozen and other cars that you might never see on the road such as a 1950's D-Type Jaguar race car similar to the one that sold at Sotheby's auction in 2016 for $19.8 million... such a thrill! AND get to stand up close for a peek inside. Looking only and never touching.

Once a month - on the First Saturday - owners and spectators alike, get up early and drive to this casual gathering held in a shopping center parking lot to have their morning coffee while showing off their fine automobiles, reminiscing over the rare ones and drooling over the exotic and high-performance machines.

This multi-million dollar display of locally owned and driven vehicles can be seen for FREE year round (even in the summer). It is a morning event and usually in full swing by 7 a.m. and dispersed by 11 a.m. Go early, grab a coffee, maybe some breakfast, and stroll through an impressive gathering of 300 or more spectacular cars.

The Scottsdale Motorsports Gathering (Cars and Coffee) is currently being held in North Scottsdale on E Mayo Dr west of Scottsdale Dr/Loop 101. Check

>TOURIST

with the organizers, Scuderia Southwest, for the most recent location.

If you have a choice, schedule your visit to include the first Saturday of the month.

30. PENSKE RACE MUSEUM

Also in the North Scottsdale area, view an exciting- and FREE - display of Penske Race Cars. You can get up close and personal to these impressive machines that were actually on the tracks and took the checkered flags.

Pick up a T-shirt, miniature replica toy car, or an autographed car part at the boutique where you will find a selection of Penske Racing merchandise and museum souvenirs.

Open daily, check for specific hours. Located at the Penske Automall at 7125 East Chauncey Lane, Phoenix

31. MORE CARS AT THE PAVILIONS

Still looking for cars? Head to The Pavilions.

If you miss the first Saturday 'Cars and Coffee', or if you want to double dip that day, take yourself to The Pavilions at Talking Stick.

Here you will see a broader collection of vehicles including classic cars and motorcycles, street and muscle cars along with the exotic and high-performance vehicles. A fun 50's era theme with music keeps the evening lively.

The Pavillions is one of the first shopping centers to be built in Scottsdale and is also one of the first locations where car buffs began gathering with their vehicles for an informal and unofficial 'show,' just sharing their love and enjoyment of their 'rides.'

This gathering happens EVERY Saturday year round at The Pavilions - rain (in Arizona?) or shine (high heat). Beginning about 4 p.m. you might see upwards of 300-500 cars by close at 8 p.m. This time you can grab a bite to eat at one of the nearby restaurants before, during or after wandering through the vehicles on display.

>TOURIST

The Pavillions at Talking Stick Shopping Center is located west of the 101/Pima Fwy on Talking Stick Way/E Indian Bend Rd

32. HORSEPOWER OF THE FOUR-LEGGED KIND

Since 1955, the annual Scottsdale Arabian Horse Show has attracted
horse lovers of all ages. I am one of those, and I love all horses.
but Arabians have always been my favorites.
Imagine two thousand magnificent horses, all Purebred Arabian and Half-Arabian horses from around the world, in Scottsdale. Talk about horsepower! It is a magical time for anyone who loves horses. These fantastic animals compete in different events for a chance to win top prizes as well as recognition for their owners, trainers, and breeders.

In addition to thousands of beautiful horses, the show offers exhibitions, demonstrations, contests and over 300 vendors.

33. MACDONALD'S RANCH

Go West? Wait!... Go North! For a real western adventure awaiting kids of all ages and great fun for the whole family, go north to MacDonald's Ranch.

Located in North Scottsdale - waaay north - on N Scottsdale Rd and E Jomax Rd, (about 5 miles north of AZ State Route 101) this historic family-owned ranch offers visitors a taste of the old west with horses and cows, stagecoaches, and trail rides, hayrides, and cookouts. Horseback riding lessons, and trail rides are available for everyone - no experience needed.

I am a fan of evening rides. Sunsets and full moons in the desert are spectacular, especially from horseback during a trail ride through the chaparral and mesquite.

Visit the old western town with a general store, petting zoo, and activities for all ages, some are FREE, such as complimentary pony rides for the little people. The Pumpkin Patch in October is great fun and attracts visitors from all over the Phoenix area.

Check their calendar for times and days of opening and closing. They are open almost year-round for at least some part of the day with a few exceptions.

Reservations are recommended. Group parties and special events are welcome.

34. FRESH AIR AND SUNSHINE

The climate and surrounding landscape of Scottsdale are a perfect combination for getting plenty of fresh air and sunshine. After all, that is one of the reasons you are here, right?

Hiking, biking, walking, and jogging trails abound, and there are golf courses galore. Stay in town or head to the nearby hills for a daily dose of fresh air and sunshine at any time of the year. Early morning or evening activities are best in the heat of summer for all outdoor activities. Where ever you go and whatever you are doing, if it is outside in the fresh air and sunshine, remember always to protect yourself from the sun's rays and drink plenty of water.

35. PAPAGO PARK

Papago Park is officially in Phoenix (and Tempe) and borders Scottsdale on the west at McDowell and Gavin Pkwy. It encompasses nearly 1500 acres of hills and geological formations called Papago Buttes.

The park provides hiking and biking trails, rock climbing and even a view of the Greater Phoenix Area through the 'Hole-in-the-Rock,' a major landmark.

An easy trail leads to the north side of one of the red sandstone buttes where an easy climb takes you to the 'Hole-in-the-Rock,' which was formed over time by erosion. I am happy to take in the panoramic view from within the 'hole.' Braver hikers than myself climb on through and out onto the smooth slope of rocks below or back up and over to another side. The hike is easy; the view is breathtaking.

Other buttes in the park have trails as well. Playgrounds, bike paths, and an 18-hole championship golf course are scattered throughout the park. Picnic grounds and man-made ponds provide a serene spot for relaxing either before, after or even instead of a fun hike, climb or a round of golf.

The Phoenix Zoo, Desert Botanical Gardens and Hunt's Tomb—the burial place of Governor George Hunt, the first governor of Arizona, and his family—are also within Papago Park. Lsted on the National Register of Historic Places, Hunt's Tomb is a white pyramid within a fence on a hill overlooking the zoo and can be spotted easily from miles around.

>TOURIST

36. DESERT BOTANICAL GARDENS

Within Papago Park on the west side of Scottsdale, the Desert Botanical Gardens is a fascinating collection and extensive landscape of desert plants from around the world. This enchanting desert garden offers walking paths and trails leading you through a variety of themed landscapes and special exhibits. Watch for native animals and birds such as rabbits, tortoises, and ground squirrels; and hummingbirds, grackles, verdins, and finches. You might even catch sight of a roadrunner!

For a different experience, visit the Gardens at night. Flashlight Tours during the summer are especially fun. Although geared toward younger visitors, I find them fascinating and quite educational. There are also evenings of music and performers.

Special exhibits, festivals and seasonal events, as well as visiting artists and sculptors, contribute to the delightful experiences in the Gardens.

I like to visit the twice-yearly Butterfly Exhibit during their spring hatch and fall migration.

Even though I am not a fan of spicy foods, I have fun at the annual Chilis and Chocolate Festival in November. The tantalizing aroma of roasting green chilis wafting through the gardens leads you to vendors offer samples and selling foods - including chocolates - flavored or infused with chilis.

My favorite event is the magical holiday celebration of Los Noches de las Luminarias. Every night during December (except December 24 & 25th) the pathways, trails, and rooftops throughout the Gardens are lined with traditional Southwestern hand-lit Luminarias - lanterns made of paper bags holding a candle and weighted down with sand. The lantern-lit paths lead to various locations throughout the Gardens where dancers, singers, musicians and story-tellers perform.

While at the Gardens, visit the gift shop with its unique selection of specialized items, some from local artists.

And eat at Gertrude's.

Access the Desert Botanic Gardens from the round-about on Gavin Pkwy south of McDowell. The second Tuesday of the month is FREE, and Dogs get to visit on special days just for them.

>TOURIST

37. GERTRUDE'S AT THE GARDENS

The Desert Botanic Gardens offers a few dining options. I enjoy Gertrudes. It is a bit pricey but the food is elegant as well as delicious, and the atmosphere is especially pleasant. Everything I've eaten at Gertrude's has been quite tasty; however, I prefer the brunch menu and especially enjoy being in the Gardens in the morning. Not hungry? Have one of their unique teas or seltzers as a refreshment during your visit. All ingredients are fresh and sourced directly from farmers around Arizona and the Southwest.

Gertrude's is near the entrance to the Gardens, next to the gift shop.

38. INDIAN BEND WASH

In the desert, a 'wash' is a place water flows from a storm in higher elevations - hills or mountains - seeking a lower elevation where it slows and eventually joins a river or lake. Over eons of time and many storms, a 'wash' - also referred to as a gully and in the southwest, an arroyo - is formed, becoming natural floodplain.

Such is the origin of Indian Bend Wash. Still 'flowing' on the east side of Scottsdale from the north (a slightly higher elevation) to the south, heading for the Salt River, Indian Bend Wash is disguised in/as a lovely greenbelt of pathways, parks, lakes and golf courses.

As a world-renown flood control project, Indian Bend Wash Greenbelt is a creative use of a recreation area doubling as a collection??.... Designed to capture/contain potentially dangerous flood water during those severe but rare desert rainstorms, Indian Bend Wash also gets to be a popular recreational area in a ..??

Flowing 11 miles through Scottsdale with underpasses at major roads, you can travel the distance without crossing high traffic roads. An excellent ride for serious long-distance bikers with connections to other trails. It is a nice family trail as well as with picnic area, skate parks, and playgrounds. Begin anywhere along the length and ride as far as desired.

Indian Bend Wash Greenbelt is a beautiful location in town for riding, walking, and jogging. I enjoy it for the parks, lakes, and wildlife - a true oasis in the desert.

>TOURIST

39. SINGH MEADOWS

Smack in the middle of the desert is a Farmers Market offering fresh locally sourced organic produce grown in Arizona; most of it right here in Scottsdale just a mile or so away.

Outgrowing their location in Scottsdale, the Singhs acquired this former golf course located at the southern end of the Scottsdale Greenbelt (Indian Bend Wash Greenbelt). The farmer's market portion of the farm was relocated here and became Singh Meadows. I love this transformation of the lower floodplain and former golf course into a peaceful 'meadow.'

After (or before) shopping the Farmers Market you'll want to linger and enjoy a refreshing drink from the juice bar, a bite to eat at the cafe (try the Biscuit and Honey - oh my!). Stay and play, take a walk, visit the pond, fly a kite toss a ball, or just lay in the grass on a complimentary blanket from one of the baskets. Pets are welcome outside in the meadow.

Purchase organic produce, artisan bread, and fresh goat cheese for a picnic or order from the café.

You will find Singh Meadows tucked back off the road where McClintock Rd (Tempe) and N

Hayden Rd (Scottsdale) merge - officially 1490 East Weber Drive, Tempe, AZ.

Open Friday - Sunday from 8 a.m. - 2 p.m.

40. HIKING, BIKING, AND HORSEBACK RIDING

Venturing from the refined urban areas of Scottsdale and somewhat level playgrounds of paths and trails, you will discover exciting opportunities for even more outdoor recreation with challenging trails for hiking, biking, and even horseback riding when you head for the hills.

Scottsdale McDowell Sonoran Preserve is a sustainable desert habitat and is open to the public for outdoor recreation. Over 180 miles of intersecting trails are open year-round from sunrise to sunset with free access. Dogs are welcome on the trails in the preserve. They must be leashed and cleaned up after.

Pinnacle Peak Park is a popular hiking destination in Scottsdale with easy accessibility, groomed trails, and beautiful scenery. The trail is considered a moderate hike and appropriate for most hikers. Bicycles are not allowed on the trail, but bike racks are available at the trailhead for securing your bicycle

>TOURIST

while you are on the trail. Dogs are not allowed on the trail, and neither are motorized vehicles.

Camelback Mountain borders Scottsdale to the west and is popular for 'in-town' hiking and rock climbing. It has two hiking trails for avid hikers. These are reputed to be strenuous trails and worth the views. The trails are a dog-friendly, but be aware of rough conditions and have plenty of water for you and your dog.

Not an avid hiker, I prefer the less strenuous hikes in Papago Park and walking along the Arizona Canal paths through Indian Bend Wash or around Singh Meadows.

41. SCOTTSDALE WATERFRONT

The Arizona Canal cuts through Scottsdale carrying precious water from the Salt River west across the valley. It is an integral part of the establishment of communities in the valley, including Scottsdale.

The banks of the canal have been developed and improved and are offer miles and miles of interactive trails, popular with walkers, joggers, bikers, and even horseback riders along some sections. Leashed dogs are welcome along the Arizona Canal Trail.

The Arizona canal has become a focal point in the expansion and development of the area of Scottsdale and Camelback Roads, crossing where the two roads intersect. With the completion of the pedestrian bridge designed by Paolo Soleri, the Scottsdale Waterfront developed into a stylish place to live, visit, and shop. Waterfront is a unique mixed-use development of high-rise residential buildings, office and retail spaces, including unique dining and drinking establishments.

Using the appeal of the canal, Scottsdale Waterfront blends into the Fashion Square Shopping area with additional retail and restaurants along the canal.

The banks of the canal through Waterfront are a popular venue for strolling, eating, drinking, and shopping, much like Old Town with a little more sophistication.

>TOURIST

42. SCOTTSDALE PUBLIC ART WALK

This is another type of Art Walk. Explore the city and discover fascinating sculptures and designs while you are out and about.

As you walk (or jog or bicycle) along the pathways of the Arizona Canal through Scottsdale, look for unique artwork enhancing the walkways, tunnels, and bridges. You will find both subtle and dramatic designs covering benches, walls, and archways, as well as creative shade structures and original sculptures.

Hint - there are about 10 or so just along the canal walkways within Scottsdale.

Go to the Scottsdale Public Art website for an interactive map and information about the pieces along the canal as well as other public art pieces around town.

43. SOLERI BRIDGE AND COPPER FALLS

Soleri Bridge and Plaza located at the southwest corner of Scottsdale and Camelback Roads is a spectacular design public art piece by Paolo Soleri, the late renowned artist, architect, and philosopher (and bronze bells and Cosani fame).

Known also for his bridge designs, this is the first and only one to be constructed which makes it even more exciting to have as a dramatic piece of art and cultural heritage in Scottsdale.

The dramatic design is both a bridge and a solar calendar which connects the elements of sun and water. The structure supporting the pedestrian passage that crosses the AZ Canal also becomes a modernistic sundial. The best time for most effect is between twelve o'clock noon and 1:00 p.m and at the solstices and equinoxes.

The plaza provides a gathering place to observe the passage of time provided by the design of the bridge. At the south end of the bridge structure is the Goldwater Bell, designed and created by Soleri.

Also at the intersection of Scottsdale Road and Camelback, is Copper Falls, another fascinating public art piece. Installed in the panels along the pedestrian bridge, copper domes of varying sizes provide unique sounds as waterfalls on them bringing the music of water to the busy street corner.

44. FUN FESTIVALS

Festivals are always fun, and Scottsdale has plenty any time of the year of them. Take your pick!

One of my favorites is the Scottsdale Arts Festival held each year in mid-March. More than an art show, it is three days of family fun bringing live music and entertainment, food, vendors and special kids'B activities together with exclusive jury-selected artists from all over the country.

Different from the fun weekly ArtWalk in Old Town which is more like a free block party, Scottsdale Arts Festival is an annual fund-raising ticketed event.

Proceeds support arts education and outreach programs, performances and exhibitions presented by Scottsdale Arts. Children under 12 are free, students and seniors get discounted prices. Single day tickets are available, but two-day passes provide a slight discount and are accepted any two of the three days.

Since food and drink are available (for purchase) at the festival, no coolers, food, or beverages, except for water, are not allowed. And NO PETS.

Scottsdale Arts Festival is at Scottsdale Civic Center Park on Drinkwater Blvd and 2nd St. There is plenty of parking, or you may take advantage of the free Scottsdale Trolley

45. CANAL CONVERGENCE

Another fun festival, that I look forward to is the exciting annual Canal Convergence at Scottsdale Waterfront. This incredible event is held each year in November for ten glorious days and nights along the Arizona Canal where it meanders through the Waterfront district just south of Fashion Square Mall at Scottsdale Rd and Camelback Rd.

This "confluence of water + art + light" is a celebration of the canal system and its influence on the growth and development of the Phoenix Valley. Hosted by Scottsdale Public Art with SRP (Salt Water Project) and the City of Scottsdale, the Canal Convergence is a fantastic experience of light displays, educational activities and interactive events, artists and exhibits, live entertainment and performances; 10 consecutive days and nights of spectacular and mesmerizing events. The best part? Admission is FREE

46. FUN AND GAMES

Bring your clubs and wear your caps! Scottsdale has long been a destination for winter visitors as well as retirees with golf at the top of their entertainment list, making this a golfer's paradise.

Even if you are attending a conference or convention, or one of the resorts is your destination, there are golf courses galore and often special package deals at some of the resorts.

Baseball is another sport that has been taking advantage of the gorgeous weather in the greater Phoenix area since the early days - as early as 1947! Wear your baseball cap, sit in the stands, eat some peanut and Cracker Jacks (now it is more like plain popcorn, hotdogs and a beer!) and watch the action!

47. PHOENIX OPEN IN SCOTTSDALE

Every year in January-February, Scottsdale is host to the annual Phoenix Open, one of the first stops on the PGA tour. Officially, this tournament is "The Waste Management Phoenix Open at TPC Scottsdale," but locally we refer to it simply as the Phoenix Open. But it is held in Scottsdale!

You don't have to be a golfer or even much of a fan to have fun at this event. It is a wonderful opportunity to catch some rays, enjoy the fresh air and watch a bit of action.

Follow the game from hole to hole or stake your claim, sit back and watch the participants play on through.

Unique to the Phoenix Open, the noise of the crowd is allowed if not encouraged at the famous 16th hole which is surrounded by seats in a coliseum-style viewing.

Check for Free General Admission during the week, compliments of Ford Free Days. Admission is free for children (17 and under) accompanied by an adult

>TOURIST

48. BASEBALL BUZZ

Loyal baseball fans already know about Spring Training in Arizona, and getting to watch their favorite teams and players get in shape for the season. But if you are less than devoted to baseball, you might not be aware of the fun and games to be had in Scottsdale during the spring training season.

Scottsdale is home to the San Francisco Giants who play right downtown at the Scottsdale Stadium on E Osborn Rd and Drinkwater Blvd. Watch the Colorado Rockies and Arizona Diamondbacks play at the Salt River Fields at Talking Stick a short distance north.

Other major teams have stadiums located around the Valley which is literally abuzz with baseball as players, recruits and fans of all the major teams swarm in for practice and exhibition games before the summer season.

Locals are found playing hooky from work or taking a long lunch to attend games. Tickets are relatively easy to acquire and reasonably priced for some fun afternoon and evening baseball action

The 'buzz' begins in February.

49. SKYSONG

At the corner of McDowell Rd and Scottsdale Rd, you might catch a glimpse of the futuristic white shade structure at SkySong, the ASU Scottsdale Innovation Center. A striking and captivating sight and one of the most recognized icons in Scottsdale, this dramatic structure is being enveloped by the ongoing expansion of the mixed-use project of commercial and retail space, restaurants, hotels, and apartments.

SkySong is a type of think-tank environment, a place where startups, as well as established technology and cutting-edge companies, collaborate and interface with resources through ASU (Arizona State University) creating opportunities for new businesses

50. HOT TIMES COOL FUN

Even in the heat of summer, you can enjoy a great vacation in Scottsdale. Early morning or late evening activities are enjoyable.

As the heat rises, the rates drop at hotels and resort. Special summer rates seasonal discounts are often available at other venues as well such as museums, theaters, galleries, golf courses and such. Misting systems help cool off patios at outdoor eating and drinking venues.

The best thing to do in the summer heat is to be in the water. Some of us locals take advantage of resort offerings and have 'Staycations' and enjoying lovely pools, water parks, lazy rivers, and water slides and poolside pampering. The 'dive-in' movies are awesome!

Golf courses abound and can be played in the cooler early morning hours. During the heat of the day, head inside for extra spa treatments and relaxation. Scottsdale is known to have the highest number of destination spas of any city in the United States

Or head into the malls for some cool shopping with air conditioning and summer sales. Outside malls like Scottsdale Quarter and Kierland Commons have some shaded walkways, misters on covered patios and of course, air conditioning in all the stores!

The is a great time to visit the indoor attractions like OdySea Aquarium and the Butterfly Pavillion - hours of airconditioned entertainment and few crowds than in the winter!

Or go for the gambling - Talking Stick Casino in the north off Hwy 101 at Talking Stick Way and Casino Arizona in the South off Hwy 101 at McKellips - for more inside air-conditioned entertainment!

>TOURIST

TOP REASONS TO BOOK THIS TRIP

Sunshine: 300 plus days a year.

Food and Drink: Top eateries, bars, pubs, and coffee houses - more than you can experience

Art and Culture: Museums, Galleries, Public Art

>TOURIST

BONUS BOOK

50 THINGS TO KNOW ABOUT PACKING LIGHT FOR TRAVEL

PACK THE RIGHT WAY EVERY TIME

AUTHOR: MANIDIPA BHATTACHARYYA

First Published in 2015 by Dr. Lisa Rusczyk. Copyright 2015. All Rights Reserved. No part of this publication may be reproduced, including scanning and photocopying, or distributed in any form or by any means, electronic or mechanical, or stored in a database or retrieval system without prior written permission from the publisher.

Disclaimer: The publisher has put forth an effort in preparing and arranging this book. The information provided herein by the author is provided "as is". Use this information at your own risk. The publisher is not a licensed doctor. Consult your doctor before engaging in any medical activities. The publisher and author disclaim any liabilities for any loss of profit or commercial or personal damages resulting from the information contained in this book.

Edited by Melanie Howthorne

ABOUT THE AUTHOR

Manidipa Bhattacharyya is a creative writer and editor, with an education in English literature and Linguistics. After working in the IT industry for seven long years she decided to call it quits and follow her heart instead. Manidipa has been ghost writing, editing, proof reading and doing secondary research services for many story tellers and article writers for about three years. She stays in Kolkata, India with her husband and a busy two year old. In her own time Manidipa enjoys travelling, photography and writing flash fiction.

Manidipa believes in travelling light and never carries anything that she couldn't haul herself on a trip. However, travelling with her child changed the scenario. She seemed to carry the entire world with her for the baby on the first two trips. But good sense prevailed and she is again working her way to becoming a light traveler, this time with a kid.

INTRODUCTION

*He who would travel happily
must travel light.*

-Antoine de Saint-Exupéry

Travel takes you to different places from seas and mountains to deserts and much more. In your travels you get to interact with different people and their cultures. You will, however, enjoy the sights and interact positively with these new people even more, if you are travelling light.

When you travel light your mind can be free from worry about your belongings. You do not have to spend precious vacation time waiting for your luggage to arrive after a long flight. There is be no chance of your bags going missing and the best part is that you need not pay a fee for checked baggage.

People who have mastered this art of packing light will root for you to take only one carry-on, wherever you go. However, many people can find it really hard to pack light. More so if you are travelling with children. Differentiating between "must have" and "just in case" items is the starting point. There will be ample shopping avenues at your destination which are just waiting to be explored.

This book will show you 'packing' in a new 'light' – pun intended – and help you to embrace light packing practices for all of your future travels.

Off to packing!

DEDICATION

I dedicate this book to all the travel buffs that I know, who have given me great insights into the contents of their backpacks.

THE RIGHT TRAVEL GEAR

1. CHOOSE YOUR TRAVEL GEAR CAREFULLY

While selecting your travel gear, pick items that are light weight, durable and most importantly, easy to carry. There are cases with wheels so you can drag them along – these are usually on the heavy side because of the trolley. Alternatively a backpack that you can carry comfortably on your back, or even a duffel bag that you can carry easily by hand or sling across your body are also great options. Whatever you choose, one thing to keep in mind is that the luggage itself should not weigh a ton, this will give you the flexibility to bring along one extra pair of shoes if you so desire.

2. CARRY THE MINIMUM NUMBER OF BAGS

Selecting light weight luggage is not everything. You need to restrict the number of bags you carry as well. One carry-on size bag is ideal for light travel. Most carriers allow one cabin baggage plus one purse, handbag or camera bag as long as it slides under the seat in front. So technically, you can carry two items of luggage without checking them in.

3. PACK ONE EXTRA BAG

Always pack one extra empty bag along with your essential items. This could be a very light weight duffel bag or even a sturdy tote bag which takes up minimal space. In the event that you end up buying a lot of souvenirs, you already have a handy bag to stuff all that into and do not have to spend time hunting for an appropriate bag.

I'm very strict with my packing and have everything in its right place. I never change a rule. I hardly use anything in the hotel room. I wheel my own wardrobe in and that's it.

Charlie Watts

CLOTHES & ACCESSORIES

4. PLAN AHEAD

Figure out in advance what you plan to do on your trip. That will help you to pick that one dress you need for the occasion. If you are going to attend a wedding then you have to carry formal wear. If not, you can ditch the gown for something lighter that will be comfortable during long walks or on the beach.

5. WEAR THAT JACKET

Remember that wearing items will not add extra luggage for your air travel. So wear that bulky jacket that you plan to carry for your trip. This saves space and can also help keep you warm during the chilly flight.

6. MIX AND MATCH

Carry clothes that can be interchangeably used to reinvent your look. Find one top that goes well with a couple of pairs of pants or skirts. Use tops, shirts and jackets wisely along with other accessories like a scarf or a stole to create a new look.

7. CHOOSE YOUR FABRIC WISELY

Stuffing clothes in cramped bags definitely takes its toll which results in wrinkles. It is best to carry wrinkle free, synthetic clothes or merino tops. This will eliminate the need for that small iron you usually bring along.

8. DITCH CLOTHES PACK UNDERWEAR

Pack more underwear and socks. These are the things that will give you a fresh feel even if you do not get a chance to wear fresh clothes. Moreover these are easy to wash and can be dried inside the hotel room itself.

9. CHOOSE DARK OVER LIGHT

While picking your clothes choose dark coloured ones. They are easy to colour coordinate and can last longer before needing a wash. Accidental food spills and dirt from the road are less visible on darker clothes.

10. WEAR YOUR JEANS

Take only one pair of Jeans with you, which you should wear on the flight. Remember to pick a pair that can be worn for sightseeing trips and is equally eloquent for dinner. You can add variety by adding light weight cargoes and chinos.

11. CARRY SMART ACCESSORIES

The right accessory can give you a fresh look even with the same old dress. An intelligent neck-piece, a couple of bright scarves, stoles or a sarong can be used in a number of ways to add variety to your clothing. These light weight beauties can double up as a nursing cover, a light blanket, beach wear, a modesty cover for visiting places of worship, and also makes for an enthralling game of peek-a-boo.

12. LEARN TO FOLD YOUR GARMENTS

Seasoned travellers all swear by rolling their clothes for compact and wrinkle free packing. Bundle packing, where you roll the clothes around a central object as if tying it up, is also a popular method of compact and wrinkle free packing. Stacking folded clothes one on top of another is a big no-no as it makes creases extreme and they are difficult to get rid of without ironing.

13. WASH YOUR DIRTY LAUNDRY

One of the ways to avoid carrying loads of clothes is to wash the clothes you carry. At some places you might get to use the laundry services or a Laundromat but if you are in a pinch, best solution is to wash them yourself. If that is the plan then carrying quick drying clothes is highly recommended, which most often also happen to be the wrinkle free variety.

14. LEAVE THOSE TOWELS BEHIND

Regular towels take up a lot of space, are heavy and take ages to dry out. If you are staying at hotels they will provide you with towels anyway. If you are travelling to a remote place, where the availability of towels look doubtful, carry a light weight travel towel of viscose material to do the job.

15. USE A COMPRESSION BAG

Compression bags are getting lots of recommendation now days from regular travellers. These are useful for saving space in your luggage when you have to pack bulky dresses. While packing for the return trip, get help from the hotel staff to arrange a vacuum cleaner.

FOOTWEAR

16. PUT ON YOUR HIKING BOOTS

If you have plans to go hiking or trekking during your trip, you will need those bulky hiking boots. The best way to carry them is to wear them on flight to save space and luggage weight. You can remove the boots once inside and be comfortable in your socks.

17. PICKING THE RIGHT SHOES

Shoes are often the bulkiest items, along with being the dainty if you are a female. They need care and take up a lot of space in your luggage. It is advisable therefore to pick shoes very carefully. If you plan to do a lot of walking and site seeing, then wearing a pair of comfortable walking shoes are a must. For more formal occasions you can carry durable, light weight flats which will not take up much space.

18. STUFF SHOES

If you happen to pack a pair of shoes, ensure you utilize their hollow insides. Tuck small items like rolled up socks or belts to save space. They will also be easy to find.

TOILETRIES

19. STASHING TOILETRIES

Carry only absolute necessities. Airline rules dictate that for one carry-on bag, liquids and gels must be in 3.4 ounce (100ml) bottles or less, and must be packed in a one quart zip-lock bag. If you are planning to stay in a hotel, the basic things will be provided for you. It's best is to buy the rest from the local market at your destination.

20. TAKE ALONG TAMPONS

Tampons are a hard to find item in a lot of countries. Figure out how many you need and pack accordingly. For longer stays you can buy them online and have them delivered to where you are staying.

21. GET PAMPERED BEFORE YOU TRAVEL

Some avid travellers suggest getting a pedicure and manicure just the day before travelling. This not only gives you a well kept look, you also save the trouble of packing nail polish. Remember, every little bit of weight reduced adds up.

ELECTRONICS

22. LUGGING ALONG ELECTRONICS

Electronics have a large role to play in our lives today. Most of us cannot imagine our lives away from our phones, laptops or tablets. However while travelling, one must consider the amount of weight these electronics add to our luggage. Thankfully smart phones come along with all the essentials tools like a camera, email access, picture editing tools and more. They are smart to the point of eliminating the need to carry multiple gadgets. Choose a smart phone that suits all your requirements and travel with the world in your palms or pocket.

23. REDUCE THE NUMBER OF CHARGERS

If you do travel with multiple electronic devices, you will have to bear the additional burden of carrying all their chargers too. Check if a single charger can be used for multiple devices. You might also consider investing in a pocket charger. These small devices support multiple devices while keeping you charged on the go.

24. TRAVEL FRIENDLY APPS

Along with smart phones come numerous apps, which are immensely helpful in our travels. You name it and you have an app for it at hand – take pictures, sharing with friends and family, torch to light dark roads, maps, checking flight/train times, find hotels and many other things. Use these smart alternatives to traditional items like books to eliminate weight and save space.

> *I get ideas about what's essential when packing my suitcase.*
>
> -Diane von Furstenberg

TRAVELLING WITH KIDS

25. BRING ALONG THE STROLLER

Kids might enjoy walking for a while but they soon tire out and a stroller is the just the right thing for them to rest in while you continue your tour. Strollers also double duty as a luggage carrier and shopping bag holder. Remember to pick a light weight, easy to handle brand of stroller. Better yet, find out in advance if you can rent a stroller at your destination.

26. BRING ONLY ENOUGH DIAPERS FOR YOUR TRIP

Diapers take up a lot of space and add to the weight of your luggage. Therefore it is advisable to carry just enough diapers to last through the trip and a few for afterwards, till you buy fresh stock at your destination. Unless of course you are travelling to a really remote area, in which case you have no choice but to carry the load. Otherwise diapers are something you will find pretty easily.

27. TAKE ONLY A COUPLE OF TOYS

Children are easily attracted by new things in their environment. While travelling they will find numerous 'new' objects to scrutinize and play with. Packing just one favorite toy is enough, or if there is no favorite toy leave out all of them in favor of stories or imaginary games.

28. CARRY KID FRIENDLY SNACKS

Create a small snack counter in your bag to store away quick bites for those sudden hunger pangs. Depending on the child's age this could include chocolates, raisins, dry fruits, granola bars or biscuits. Also keep a bottle of water handy for your little one.

These things do not add much weight and can be adjusted in a handbag or knapsack.

29. GAMES TO CARRY

Create some travel specific, imaginary games if you have slightly grown up children, like spot the attractions. Keep a coloring book and colors handy for in-flight or hotel time. Apps on your smart phone can keep the children engaged with cartoons and story books. Older children are often entertained by games available on phones or tablets. This cuts the weight of luggage down while keeping the kids entertained.

30. LET THE KIDS CARRY THEIR LOAD

A good thing is to start early sharing of responsibilities. Let your child pick a bag of his or her choice and pack it themselves. Keep tabs on what they are stuffing in their bags by asking if they will be using that item on the trip. It could start out being just an entertainment bag initially but with growing years they will learn to sort the useful from the superfluous. Children as little as four can maneuver a small trolley suitcase like a pro- their experience in pull along toys credit. If you are worried that you may be pulling it for them, you may want to start with a backpack.

31. DECIDE ON LOCATION FOR CHILDREN TO SLEEP

While on a trip you might not always get a crib at your destination, and carrying one will make life all the more difficult. Instead call ahead to see if there are any cribs or roll out beds for children. You may even put blankets on the floor. Weave them a story about camping and they will gladly sleep without any trouble.

32. GET BABY PRODUCTS DELIVERED AT YOUR DESTINATION

If you are absolutely paranoid about not getting your favourite variety of diaper or brand of baby food, check out online stores like amazon.com for services in your destination city. You can buy things online ahead of your travel and get them delivered to your hotel upon arrival.

33. FEEDING NEEDS OF YOUR INFANTS

If you are travelling with a breastfed infant, you save the trouble of carrying bottles and bottle sanitization kits. For special food, or medications, you may need to call ahead to make sure you have a refrigerator where you are staying.

34. FEEDING NEEDS OF YOUR TODDLER

With the progression from infancy to toddler, their dietary requirements too evolve. You will have to pack some snacks for travelling time. Fresh fruits and vegetables can be purchased at your destination. Most of the cities you travel to in whichever part of the world, will have baby food products and formulas, available at the local drug-store or the supermarket.

35. PICKING CLOTHES FOR YOUR BABY

Contrary to popular belief, babies can do without many changes of clothes. At the most pack 2 outfits per day. Pack mix and match type clothes for your little one as well. Pick things which are comfortable to wear and quick to dry.

36. SELECTING SHOES FOR YOUR BABY

Like outfits, kids can make do with two pairs of comfortable shoes. If you can get some water resistant shoes it will be best. To expedite drying wet shoes, you can stuff newspaper in them then wrap them with newspaper and leave them to dry overnight.

37. KEEP ONE CHANGE OF CLOTHES HANDY

Travelling with kids can be tricky. Keep a change of clothes for the kids and mum handy in your purse or tote bag. This takes a bit of space in your hand luggage but comes extremely handy in case there are any accidents or spills.

38. LEAVE BEHIND BABY ACCESSORIES

Baby accessories like their bed, bath tub, car seat, crib etc. should be left at home. Many hotels provide a crib on request, while car seats can be borrowed from friends or rented. Babies can be given a bath in the hotel sink or even in the adult bath tub with a little bit of water. If you bring a few bath toys, they can be used in the bath, pool, and out of water. They can also be sanitized easily in the sink.

39. CARRY A SMALL LOAD OF PLASTIC BAGS

With children around there are chances of a number of soiled clothes and diapers. These plastic bags help to sort the dirt from the clean inside your big bag.

>TOURIST

These are very light weight and come in handy to other carry stuff as well at times.

PACK WITH A PURPOSE

40. PACKING FOR BUSINESS TRIPS

One neutral-colored suit should suffice. It can be paired with different shirts, ties and accessories for different occasions. One pair of black suit pants could be worn with a matching jacket for the office or with a snazzy top for dinner.

41. PACKING FOR A CRUISE

Most cruises have formal dinners, and that formal dress usually takes up a lot of space. However you might find a tuxedo to rent. For women, a short black dress with multiple accessory options will do the trick.

42. PACKING FOR A LONG TRIP OVER DIFFERENT CLIMATES

The secret packing mantra for travel over multiple climates is layering. Layering traps air around your body creating insulation against the cold. The same light t-shirt that is comfortable in a warmer climate can be the innermost layer in a colder climate.

REDUCE SOME MORE WEIGHT

43. LEAVE PRECIOUS THINGS AT HOME

Things that you would hate to lose or get damaged leave them at home. Precious jewelry, expensive gadgets or dresses, could be anything. You will not require these on your trip. Leave them at home and spare the load on your mind.

44. SEND SOUVENIRS BY MAIL

If you have spent all your money on purchasing souvenirs, carrying them back in the same bag that you brought along would be difficult. Either pack everything in another bag and check it in the airport or get everything shipped to your home. Use an international carrier for a secure transit, but this could be more expensive than the checking fees at the airport.

45. AVOID CARRYING BOOKS

Books equal to weight. There are many reading apps which you can download on your smart phone or tab.

Plus there are gadgets like Kindle and Nook that are thinner and lighter alternatives to your regular book.

CHECK, GET, SET, CHECK AGAIN

46. STRATEGIZE BEFORE PACKING

Create a travel list and prepare all that you think you need to carry along. Keep everything on your bed or floor before packing and then think through once again – do I really need that? Any item that meets this question can be avoided. Remove whatever you don't really need and pack the rest.

47. TEST YOUR LUGGAGE

Once you have fully packed for the trip take a test trip with your luggage. Take your bags and go to town for window shopping for an hour. If you enjoy your hour long trip it is good to go, if not, go home and reduce the load some more. Repeat this test till you hit the right weight.

48. ADD A ROLL OF DUCT TAPE

You might wonder why, when this book has been talking about reducing stuff, we're suddenly asking you to pack something totally unusual. This is because when you have limited supplies, duct tape is immensely helpful for small repairs – a broken bag, leaking zip-lock bag, broken sunglasses, you name it and duct tape can fix it, temporarily.

49. LIST OF ESSENTIAL ITEMS

Even though the emphasis is on packing light, there are things which have to be carried for any trip. Here is our list of essentials:

- Passport/Visa or any other ID

- Any other paper work that might be required on a trip like permits, hotel reservation confirmations etc.

- Medicines – all your prescription medicines and emergency kit, especially if you are travelling with children

- Medical or vaccination records

- Money in foreign currency if travelling to a different country

- Tickets- Email or Message them to your phone

50. MAKE THE MOST OF YOUR TRIP

Wherever you are going, whatever you hope to do we encourage you to embrace it whole-heartedly. Take in the scenery, the culture and above all, enjoy your time away from home.

On a long journey even a straw weighs heavy.

-Spanish Proverb

>TOURIST

PACKING AND PLANNING TIPS

A Week before Leaving

- Arrange for someone to take care of pets and water plants.
- Stop mail and newspaper.
- Notify Credit Card companies where you are going.
- Change your thermostat settings.
- Car inspected, oil is changed, and tires have the correct pressure.
- Passports and photo identification is up to date.
- Pay bills.
- Copy important items and download travel Apps.
- Start collecting small bills for tips.

Right Before Leaving

- Clean out refrigerator.
- Empty garbage cans.
- Lock windows.
- Make sure you have the proper identification with you.
- Bring cash for tips.
- Remember travel documents.
- Lock door behind you.
- Remember wallet.
- Unplug items in house and pack chargers.

>TOURIST

READ OTHER GREATER THAN A TOURIST BOOKS

Greater Than a Tourist San Miguel de Allende Guanajuato Mexico: 50 Travel Tips from a Local by Tom Peterson

Greater Than a Tourist – Lake George Area New York USA: 50 Travel Tips from a Local by Janine Hirschklau

Greater Than a Tourist – Monterey California United States: 50 Travel Tips from a Local by Katie Begley

Greater Than a Tourist – Chanai Crete Greece: 50 Travel Tips from a Local by Dimitra Papagrigoraki

Greater Than a Tourist – The Garden Route Western Cape Province South Africa: 50 Travel Tips from a Local by Li-Anne McGregor van Aardt

Greater Than a Tourist – Sevilla Andalusia Spain: 50 Travel Tips from a Local by Gabi Gazon

Greater Than a Tourist – Kota Bharu Kelantan Malaysia: 50 Travel Tips from a Local by Aditi Shukla

Children's Book: Charlie the Cavalier Travels the World by Lisa Rusczyk

>TOURIST

> TOURIST

Visit Greater Than a Tourist for Free Travel Tips
http://GreaterThanATourist.com

Sign up for the Greater Than a Tourist Newsletter for discount days, new books, and travel information:
http://eepurl.com/cxspyf

Follow us on Facebook for tips, images, and ideas:
https://www.facebook.com/GreaterThanATourist

Follow us on Pinterest for travel tips and ideas:
http://pinterest.com/GreaterThanATourist

Follow us on Instagram for beautiful travel images:
http://Instagram.com/GreaterThanATourist

>TOURIST

> TOURIST

Please leave your honest review of this book on Amazon and Goodreads. Please send your feedback to GreaterThanaTourist@gmail.com as we continue to improve the series. We appreciate your positive and constructive feedback. Thank you.

METRIC CONVERSIONS

TEMPERATURE

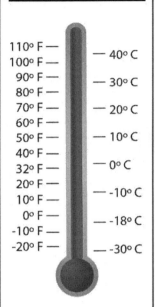

To convert F to C:

Subtract 32, and then multiply by 5/9 or .5555.

To Convert C to F:

Multiply by 1.8 and then add 32.

32F = 0C

LIQUID VOLUME

To Convert:.................Multiply by
U.S. Gallons to Liters................ 3.8
U.S. Liters to Gallons 26
Imperial Gallons to U.S. Gallons 1.2
Imperial Gallons to Liters....... 4.55
Liters to Imperial Gallons 22
1 Liter = .26 U.S. Gallon
1 U.S. Gallon = 3.8 Liters

DISTANCE

To convert ....Multiply by
Inches to Centimeters 2.54
Centimeters to Inches 39
Feet to Meters...................... .3
Meters to Feet 3.28
Yards to Meters 91
Meters to Yards 1.09
Miles to Kilometers 1.61
Kilometers to Miles............ .62
1 Mile = 1.6 km
1 km = .62 Miles

WEIGHT

1 Ounce = .28 Grams
1 Pound = .4555 Kilograms
1 Gram = .04 Ounce
1 Kilogram = 2.2 Pounds

>TOURIST

TRAVEL QUESTIONS

- Do you bring presents home to family or friends after a vacation?
- Do you get motion sick?
- Do you have a favorite billboard?
- Do you know what to do if there is a flat tire?
- Do you like a sun roof open?
- Do you like to eat in the car?
- Do you like to wear sun glasses in the car?
- Do you like toppings on your ice cream?
- Do you use public bathrooms?
- Did you bring your cell phone and does it have power?
- Do you have a form of identification with you?
- Have you ever been pulled over by a cop?
- Have you ever given money to a stranger on a road trip?
- Have you ever taken a road trip with animals?
- Have you ever went on a vacation alone?
- Have you ever run out of gas?

- If you could move to any place in the world, where would it be?
- If you could travel anywhere in the world, where would you travel?
- If you could travel in any vehicle, which one would it be?
- If you had three things to wish for from a magic genie, what would they be?
- If you have a driver's license, how many times did it take you to pass the test?
- What are you the most afraid of on vacation?
- What do you want to get away from the most when you are on vacation?
- What foods smells bad to you?
- What item do you bring on ever trip with you away from home?
- What makes you sleepy?
- What song would you love to hear on the radio when you're cruising on the highway?
- What travel job would you want the least?
- What will you miss most while you are away from home?
- What is something you always wanted to try?

>TOURIST

- What is the best road side attraction that you ever saw?
- What is the farthest distance you ever biked?
- What is the farthest distance you ever walked?
- What is the weirdest thing you needed to buy while on vacation?
- What is your favorite candy?
- What is your favorite color car?
- What is your favorite family vacation?
- What is your favorite food?
- What is your favorite gas station drink or food?
- What is your favorite license plate design?
- What is your favorite restaurant?
- What is your favorite smell?
- What is your favorite song?
- What is your favorite sound that nature makes?
- What is your favorite thing to bring home from a vacation?
- What is your favorite vacation with friends?
- What is your favorite way to relax?

- Where is the farthest place you ever traveled in a car?
- Where is the farthest place you ever went North, South, East and West?
- Where is your favorite place in the world?
- Who is your favorite singer?
- Who taught you how to drive?
- Who will you miss the most while you are away?
- Who if the first person you will contact when you get to your destination?
- Who brought you on your first vacation?
- Who likes to travel the most in your life?
- Would you rather be hot or cold?
- Would you rather drive above, below, or at the speed limited?
- Would you rather drive on a highway or a back road?
- Would you rather go on a train or a boat?
- Would you rather go to the beach or the woods?

>TOURIST

TRAVEL BUCKET LIST

1.

2.

3.

4.

5.

6.

7.

8.

9.

10.

>TOURIST NOTES

Made in United States
Orlando, FL
15 November 2023